No Title, No Chapters
Words from
The 21st Century
Shakespearean Poet

Stewart Marshall Gulley

I dedicate this book to thy soul,

for It requires one to listen.

ne evening in 2007, something came over me that caused me to write. As a down-home country person, I began to write Shakespeare. People said I was channeling, but to me, I was just in tune with the divine. I did not study Shakespeare in school, nor was I an English major. For 25 years I was a hairstylist/barber. One evening in 2000, I was in the salon alone. Becoming tired of the beauty business, I knew there was something more. I stood there and asked God what was in me and what should I do. The answer came to me that I was a writer, so I literally believed it. Within a month's time, I had closed the shop down and challenged God to see if He knew what He was talking about. I lived off a charge card to pay my house note for a year. That first year I had written 5 books. Later I moved to California and continued to write. One day in March 2018, I was looking for a particular book, and I came across this manuscript that was written in a Shakespearean style. I looked at the date and one page had on it April 10, 2007, and another page had April 25, 2007-1:45 am, which was my mother's birthday. At the time of this writing, she was still living and eventually, passed away in 2010. I had no idea what I was going through while writing this, so I cannot express feelings

that caused me to write. All I know, it was divine. The only thing I could remember was writing the very last past and telling God that I didn't want to write any more of this type of language, and I wanted to stop. I stopped and went on with life as usual, writing plays and short novelettes. After 11 years, stumbling across this manuscript, I began to read and tears began to flow down my cheeks. It was something I had never experienced. You are about to read what divinely controlled my fingers and writing for 21 handwritten pages.

e thou ever present;

'Tis not the time for thou to be entangled in such place that has no value.

Why doth thou waste thy time repeatedly in encouragement? For thou has never moved from the first listening of it.

Could it be that thou are addicted to a voice of higher sound,

Yet thy mood hath left thee not knowing where it's bound?

Search inside thyself once more;

Seek in that which thou knoweth, for others gleam at wealth in others by understanding what thou showeth.

 ords of wisdom must thou hear,

But be not addicted to their thought.

For they too seek following;

Understanding what God hath wrought.

Listen to thy leader,

Only with the ear of weight.

For not every word he measures;

For he too must welcome fate.

Therefore, no one knows all the answers.

Must thought wait to hear God spake?

In due time thy darkness lighten,

And truth revealed maketh thou feel great.

etter be thou cheerful dance,

Than bowed head of heart now turns.

'Twas the grace of God pre-kissed;

Heart of warmth receives romance.

Canst thou laugh and cry at the time of even?

Separate each has its own.

The blanket is thy mind no worry;

Until pierced of the heart of thee be known.

Ever wilt thou hold up high

The name that often beckons thee.

For thy appointed time of mercy,

Shalt thou share for others free?

 arry not a strange desire.

Must thou engage in hearts unknown?

Weary will thy nights compassion

Linger for a peaceful morn.

Now that thou has ceased the moment,

Wondereth where thy passion be?

Seek, there's closer love that knocketh.

Passions lie from God in thee.

Wilt thou entangle one with madness,

O'er thou presence hinders thee?

Jus' as anger travails thy sorrow,

More thy Father sets me free.

ome now gentle one of sadness.

Doth thou know who maketh thee?

Better yet be thou with gladness;

Hast thou start so deep in thee?

Get thou strength from Spirit's dwelling,

For it lingers to beckon thee.

Wiping out thy inner sadness,

For it seeks for victory.

Tarry not for inner glory;

Wake thy morrow trouble free.

Then thou seeth in amazement,

Unanswered mysteries still set thee free.

ury not thy morrow, for thou hath not seen

The memory of thy yesterday, yet it brought not gleam.

But thy present moment, the hope of glory to travail;

Now so ever, the presence of thy God do hail.

Must thy sorrow splatter deeply

Caus' thou knoweth not yet why?

Has thy tender mercy forsaken thee?

Maybe thine don't hear thy cry.

Mercy is thy heart with laughter.

Canst thou hear a tune within thee?

Ever playing rhythm's voice;

Melodies of heart rejoicing, nesting not of thine's own choice.

 e it small or grand in echoes,

Pacing within harmony.

If thou waseth one's own moment,

Just to pause and look at thee.

Lasting tilst thou ere' rejoice;

Now thou knoweth

Why heart of gladness

Kindly respect thy own true voice.

Follow through thy lad of mercy,

Hinder not what causes thee.

Pressing toward thy heart's desire,

All respect and all to see.

 ow yet not to those unwelcomed;

Canst thou see who holds the key?

Maybe if thou slowly chasten,

Discipline wilst set thou free.

Come thy Spirit, thou hast covered

With such flesh caresses thee.

Maybe if thou choose a new presence,

Happy wilt thou ever be.

When thou feareth nature's call,

Wondereth who will discuss thee.

Better force thy loving spirit,

For God invest so much in thee.

 hanneling through new heights a calling,

Might be this one makes me free.

Every step thou taketh is willing

Just to conquer what waits on thee.

In thy corner wilst thou lay;

Burdened down by life's oppression.

Can this space become thy ending

After much hearing thy confession?

Rather sleep than face thy trouble;

Who did know thy floor would see?

Help that's far is ever waiting,

Slowly come to helpeth me.

 e ye not a traveling servant;

Much do care when seeth me.

Better thou lay cuddled closely,

Not to burn those who see.

Wilt thy last breath be untimely,

Strengthened that thou has no help to thee?

Let thy Spirit kindly beckon

With closed eyes that no more see.

Thou empowered with thy weakness.

Be it known who's mercy see;

That thou God forever giveth

Peace unknown to make men free.

estless eyes that weary timely,

For thou know what thou hath seen.

Rest upon thy fabric closely,

Tilt thou sleep as others gleam.

When thou waketh be thou grateful,

Be thou hath to honor thee.

With much time thou taketh thy presence,

Much thy flesh he gives to thee.

Be thou ever so grateful

In the midst of thine own trials.

For there seeketh one who delivers,

Traveleth close and spread thus miles.

16

hen thou delivereth me from thine oppression,

Wilt thou still find favor on me?

He doth burden others swiftly,

Yet he knoweth not yet thee.

Come now father you of many;

'Tis thy loving-kindness be.

Once again thou doth answer,

Coming soon thou set thee free.

Dancing with thy tender jollies,

Prancing free upon thy space.

Wilt thou ever more so swiftly,

Round and round enchanting grace?

 isten to thy feet who whispers;

Moves thou quickly ever see.

Doth thou stop to pause a knowing,

Catch thy breath so tenderly?

Maybe if thou question freely,

Then thou answer ever be.

Yes, thou dance the dance of wanting

Ere' to be so sacred thee.

Careth thou not of life's depression?

Doth thou know who protecteth thee?

Thou shalt dance the dance of freedom;

That's where peace encompasses thee.

 here's thy voice of yonder's gift?

Wilt thou speak to comfort thee?

There's a word enchantment's glory

Surely comes to comfort thee.

'Twas in darkness tears of pain;

Knoweth not a word from thee.

Unexpected time of presence,

Words that cometh to set me free.

Canst thou be untwined

From such an array of bliss?

For in thou moment of despair;

Wilt thy love and kindness miss?

 'er the waves of seashore be

In thy hands extended wide.

For like the wind ere' blowest free;

Forever is thy God beside.

Who doth dwell in wrath unknown?

To it be for lessons seek;

When a faulty matter dwells,

For yonder's God be also meek.

Tarry not thy kindness bow,

Let thy lovers face rejoice.

Whence thou seek the heart of peace?

Let thou hear in God's sweet voice.

ilt thou weary one embrace

Yonder voice of caring echoes?

'Tis thou ever hold the space;

Hover o'er God's precious billows.

Take thine hand extended upward,

As thou mercy sweep near thee.

Know thou canst be so mindful;

'Twas God's grace that remembered thee.

Morrow's not so ever promised,

Yet it's planned in front of thee.

When thou sit and let heart ponder,

Many seek door to open with key.

arry not in making haste,

For time wasted is not of thee.

While thou ever be so thankful,

Words thou push to victory.

In thy ending phrase taunt not;

Hide its tender breeze of thought.

Sharing can thou evenly echo,

Words of peace that thou hath brought.

Dark thee hour o' thy hinder;

Canst thou stop upon thee set?

No one knoweth darketh presence;

But thank thee, God not seen thee yet.

onely is thy hearts compassion,

Fester through life's open space.

Wilt thou ever greet love's entrance,

O'er for a more suspicious space?

Like thy blinded eye of mercy;

Kindled is thy beckoned cry.

No more wilt thy passion hinder,

Unveiling truth pure like thine eye.

Carry not days to thy morrow;

Too much weight for hour's fate.

Canst thou live a new enlightenment?

New day bringeth new ray's light.

itter night and sweet shine mornings;

Open eyes to thy delight.

Tender mercy of thy presence;

Thank thy God 'tis de' new light.

However be it little to be known

When time escapes and is no more.

'Twas thine life on earth must dwell,

To seek for peace upon one's shore.

And in my task to find the thread

That leads me to thy precious space.

For in it, I shall truly hail

With loving-kindness I've won the race.

ow I know why time 'twas hard;

Only to build thy gift within.

And if I knew this once ahead,

Forgive me for wanting to do again.

I do err on what I thought,

Looking for help from yonder's tree.

For I have found a branch within;

The seed of a tree begins in me.

Wilt thou ever be so mindful

Of thy kindred Spirit be?

When thou dwelleth in thy chambers,

Know thou comes to comfort thee.

here art thou who oppresses thee?

Doth thou know 'tis not a chance?

To increase thy child of mercy,

Past oppressions must regress.

Lift thy only thoughts compassion,

Hear me now whilst thou do listen.

Ever grace thy sheets of work;

Tell thy Father who hath mercy only. Wait for His thy comfort lurk.

Rest thine eye for weary art thee,

'Til morrow waits for its fate.

Sleep in kindness, peace everlasting;

Now waketh thou for mercy's sake.

 is a wonder thou doth see;

The veil of light from heights unknown.

A cast o glee betwixt thy heart;

For wonders, joy doth enter thee.

And while thy faith mix yonder's grace,

A force of love doth come to thee.

And when love cease from earth's dismay,

I know thine God is still with me.

No man hinders man's own lot,

For he must travel as he's pulled.

For when thy Spirit speaks to thine,

Thou ever be his heart will rule.

 anst thou be ever mindful

Of the lot that thine must bear?

For in it, God be known His power

That thou forever helps you share.

Never alone wilst thy master leave thee;

Know thou touch is ever near.

Remember in thou disappointments,

It is still thy God that brought us here.

Can thou water leave its wetness

Without a plan from thou on high?

'Tis the same that in our gladness

Doth thy God removes the sigh.

ow doth knowledge wilt thou seek

Where wisdom awaits thy better thoughts?

For there's an answer boldly waiting;

Forevermore doth our God wrought.

Whether be it now or later,

'Tis thy moon decrease its height.

Furthermore, art thou dwelling;

'Tis to hunger for much light.

Canst thou see without a vision,

Better yet without thy sight?

One must deepen in hearts luster

To fulfill all that's in thy might.

 owly art thy simple wonders;

Less the time we make no haste.

For thy gift art ever saddened

We do not share or honor grace.

Ever been so busy minded

That thou forget thy laws of life?

When thou seeketh other talents

That thine own should suffer strife.

So with that, I tenderly mention

In the moments of tender thought.

Ever be a willing teacher,

For with thine blood that thou hast bought.

herish not that which has no value,

Soon be it shall ever fade.

But with gladness thou shalt treasure

He who made us of glorious shade.

From the labor of thy garden's bloom;

Wilt thou taketh from thy stem

A clipping of thy heart's desire

Waiting for thy special gem?

In a pool of jasmine;

Wilt thy body caress thy water

Knowing that thy fragrance travel

Never ceasing odor's daughter?

 ead laid back amongst thy float,

Dreaming of thy upward sky.

Come, thy hither madness quickly

Awake thy dream with a kiss on thy eye.

Now that we're entangled heartly,

Let thy spirit flow within.

Ever knowing thou art equal,

Balanced love shalt thou careen.

When yonder's joy seek not to smile,

Thy tired feet can't walk thine mile;

And hungered soul no meal de' fed,

Must wonder if better yet thou dead.

 ark not thy troubled one of grace,

'Tis wonder what thy life be doom.

For labor has thy warm hands sought;

Sun up, sun down, and ever noon.

Why canst thou lift thy burdened heart?

For 'tis the time thy cancel gloom.

If God doth care with tender mercy,

Thou shalt come hither oh too soon.

Although thy body looks of travail

And clothes of weathery threads do wear,

I know from whence that thou do suffer;

For once thy soul had rested there.

ut one day thou took up the thought;

If thou be present nigh

And faith withhold the truth of light,

Thou expect thy God to answer I.

Call all good things as though they were

In acts be known to man.

And when that thou has lifted thee,

No more thy feet amongst the sand.

Glory to thy crown of wisdom,

For thou heard thy beckoned cry.

Change thy mindset toward endeavors;

Must thou never think of try?

ellow partners in this light

Of wisdom's thought;

Casting wayward all confusion.

Though, thy weakened soul has

bought.

Chide for what thou know within,

Not what some man's new thoughts placed.

But with faith and glory's forward,

Confusing thoughts that thou hast raced.

Never buy another's vision

Lest thou hast forgot his own.

Unhappy wilt thy days be numbered,

'Til thy wisdom of thine own be shown.

elp 'tis always welcomed quickly;

'Tis not wrong to lend a hand.

But without thy wisdom calling,

Conquered body no place to stand.

Days gone by and strength has weakened,

Wondereth what has taken thee.

'Twas thy generously seeking presence;

But thou had forgotten to invest in thee.

When the light of darkness hovers

O'er, thy spirit lingers nigh.

'Twas thy days so enchanting;

'Tis night winds to conquer I.

 alone lay here panting

Like an animal of thirst be known.

Catch thy breath for heart's desire;

Ever live much mercy shown.

Now that I have wilted slowly,

Youth has seen its time of woe.

Gracefully, I'll ever thank thee

Thou canst live forever more.

Dandelions, tulips dancing;

Pussy willow, roses prancing;

'Tis the season for enhancing;

Glory's bloom art quite enchanting.

 cary art thy many pleasures;

How can it be obtaineth from thee?

Toil and sweat thou many measures;

Pleasure and sweat come to thee.

Any man who slothful sweat,

Expect thou not to be so free.

He wondereth in thy morning darkness,

While there is light, but still canst see.

Choice of pleasure thou hath taken;

Now thy weary one doth see.

Still thy chance of overcoming;

But thou must learn to trust in thee.

 is thy wonder glory gleameth.

Must thy presence soon release?

Blooming lights of ever gladness;

Sacred stories to increase.

Gentle angels are thy substance;

Let thy heart spread open wide.

Next to mercy gentle kindness;

Peace on earth to thee abide.

'Tis a wonder; thine own depression

Has not cancelled out thy many years of thought.

Dwelling on past contentment,

Wilt thou ever be free with thou past hath fought?

 et thy mind seek other objectives;

Grasping for thine breath of air.

'Twas a dreamer thou has risen;

Brought to past though others not care.

Can there be a light of connection

Pondering through thy darkness glare?

Pressing toward thy greater height;

Thou in darkness no longer stare.

Grateful art thou words of wisdom,

Only to thrust thy secret thought.

Knowing that of treasure listened;

Gladly accept what thou's been taught.

 ow that dawning has approached us,

Know that thy work 'twas done.

Better work while thou art able,

Labor older 'tis no fun.

Ever be thy present mindset,

Changing to thy wisdom's door.

Must thou share what thou has glistened?

Know thy Father gives us more.

Ever be the glitch of time

That cast no dwelling place.

For thou art ever present be

In thy holding of much space.

 ore yet though in times of past,

Dealt not wisely. Hence,

For joy and peace that conquers all

When wisdom has finally circumvent.

Now dwelt thee of higher taste;

For yet thy knowledge do increase.

For now, thou hast seen thine end result,

That wisdom hath thou so soon released.

Oh, little child of mercy;

Canst thou cry for peace alone?

For thy thoughts are heavy burned;

Only oneself must bare 'til gone.

 aybe if thou encounters

New thoughts of thee on high;

Everlasting is thy wisdom,

Mercy, grace; all so nearby.

'Twas the latter thought of anger;

Beguiled was thy sincere heart.

Know that there is not one stranger,

That thy God knoweth what He imparts.

Only maketh if thou be wiser;

In thy presence, wisdom smiles.

Every past that thou encountered,

Brought you to each step and miles.

hat part of troubles did thou forget

Whence troubles came thy way?

For someone's mercy did they release

And found you hurt in thine own way.

In the stillness of thy moment,

Everlasting chiding be.

'Twas the light, 'tis the new dawning;

Grateful art thou soul to thee.

In the stillness of thy moonlight,

Moons that drip of heart's despair.

Ever seeking for true enchantment,

New love found must know one care.

ove that's altered from thine heart,

Cannot bear thy forsaken link.

Seeking the subconscious peace of mind;

Dwelling wonders obscure mind, intake justice ever speak.

Collate thy conscious thought;

Know that thou should inquire

Whether faults lie within thyself

Or others faults do not inspire.

Spake not of thy past;

What good shall it do?

Not much time to speak of any;

Speak thy future to get you through.

OTHER BOOKS:

How to Get Over a Past Relationship Faster
Than You Think (Self-Help)

Buck Naked - Stripping away the layers
of life to get to the real
you. (Self-Help)

Stay In Your Own Lane – Minding your own
business to reach your goal
(Self-Help)

It Started at 2, Not 2:15 – for people who are
always late

Eric, The Last Child – The secret that destroyed
a city may be in a neighborhood near
you! (Novel)
For Adults

Love Should Have Brought You Home Last
Night (Novelette) For Adults Only

High Heels and Bad Feet – Be careful where
you take your shoes off
(Novelette)

His Eye is on the Sparrow- Children's Coloring
& Storybook with Comprehension Test